MIND-BOGGLING
one-minute
MYSTERIES
and
BRAIN
teasers

Sandy Silverthorne & John Warner

HARVEST HOUSE PUBLISHERS

EUGENE, OREGON

Cover by Left Coast Design, Portland, Oregon
Cover illustration © Sandy Silverthorne
Back cover author photos © Milo J. Skinner

MIND-BOGGLING ONE-MINUTE MYSTERIES AND BRAIN TEASERS
Copyright © 2010 by Sandy Silverthorne and John Warner
Published by Harvest House Publishers
Eugene, Oregon 97402
www.harvesthousepublishers.com

ISBN 978-0-7369-3008-6

Printed in the United States of America

11 12 13 14 15 16 17 / VP-NI / 10 9 8 7 6 5 4

To my mom and dad—thanks for
all the encouragement and support.

And to Kristin, Jaxon, Chloe, and Ella.

John

To Vicki—you're truly the love of my life.

To Christy, my comedy partner—
thanks for your love and support.

And to Howdy and Patti—thank you
for giving me a place to be creative
and productive. You're the best.

Sandy

Thanks to Kristin Warner
for "at the Bus Stop."

Thanks to Wayne Warner
for "Lost and Not Found."

Thanks to Sandy Warner
for "Up a Tree" and "All Washed Up."

Contents

INTRODUCTION

What Are One-Minute Mysteries?

These short interactive mysteries are usually played in a group as an interactive game. You might know them as lateral thinking puzzles, yes/no puzzles, or situation puzzles. Each puzzle describes an unusual scenario, and your job is to figure out what is going on. Although the puzzles may seem open-ended, the goal is to figure out the most satisfying answer, the one that suddenly appears when the lightbulb goes off in your head and you say, "Aha!" (In other words, you're looking for a solution that matches the one in the back of the book.) Each mystery takes less than a minute to read, and then you can take your time and enjoy the sleuthing process!

How Do I Solve Them?

These puzzles don't generally provide you with enough information to find the solution, but you can fill in the gaps by asking yes-or-no questions. The solving process is similar to the game of 20 questions, but instead of finding the identity of a thing, you solve a mystery. You'll need one other person in order to enjoy these puzzles to the fullest, and the more people, the better! Choose one person to be the case master. This person reads a puzzle aloud and privately consults the answer in the back of the book. All other players are the detectives. They take turns posing questions to the case master, who can respond by saying yes or no or something like "That doesn't matter" or "Rephrase your question." The case master provides clues from the back of the book as needed. The game is won when someone figures out the key to the solution. It isn't necessary to recite the entire solution, but only to figure out the part that explains what is puzzling.

What Kind of Questions Should I Ask?

Start by asking big-picture questions. You will be tempted to jump right in and guess the answer, but you will most likely be wrong. In the game of 20 questions, you wouldn't start by guessing if the person is thinking of a tow truck. Instead, you'd get some general information first. Use the same strategy here. Give yourself something to build on by asking questions like these: Is the location important? Is anyone else involved? Could this happen to me? As you figure out what is going on, you can ask more specific questions. Also, ask completely random and off-the-wall questions. You never know what will spark some new insight!

Here is a sample puzzle and some dialogue that shows how the questioning process works:

> CASE MASTER: Bob is a delivery man, and he's in a hurry. He approaches a railroad crossing as the barriers start lowering. He won't cross the intersection before they close, but he doesn't have time to stop. What does he do?
>
> DETECTIVE: Does his speed matter?
>
> CASE MASTER: No.
>
> DETECTIVE: Does he go a different way?
>
> CASE MASTER: No.
>
> DETECTIVE: Does he drive over or under a bridge?
>
> CASE MASTER: No and no.

DETECTIVE: Does the kind of vehicle Bob is driving matter?

CASE MASTER: Yes!

DETECTIVE: Is the vehicle Bob is driving really short?

CASE MASTER: It doesn't matter.

DETECTIVE: Okay, is Bob driving an ambulance and the train stops for Bob?

CASE MASTER: No.

DETECTIVE: Um…is Bob driving something that doesn't have to stop for the railroad crossing?

CASE MASTER: Yes!

DETECTIVE: Oh! Is Bob actually driving the train himself?

CASE MASTER: Yes! Bob is driving the train, so he continues through the crossing.

Detective: That was tricky.

What Else Do I Need to Know?

1. Always check your assumptions. If a puzzle doesn't come right out and say something, don't assume it is true. Ask yourself, *What am I assuming?* If the case master can't answer one of your questions with a yes or no but instead tells you to rephrase your question, you are probably assuming something that isn't true.

2. The five senses are often important in these puzzles. Ask questions about sight, sound, touch, taste, and smell. Don't forget to check the opposite of what you initially observe. Should the person see, hear, smell, taste, or feel something that he or she can't?

3. Ask yourself who, what, when, why, how, and where. Who is involved? What is important in the puzzle? When did this occur? Is the time of day or the year important? Why did things happen this way? Does it matter where this happened? How did it happen?

4. Eliminate red herrings. Look at each element of the puzzle and ask if it is important. This way you can focus your questioning on important details.

5. Ask if you are being tricked. Many times these puzzles aren't as straightforward as they seem and are actually leading you to believe something that isn't true.

6. Think laterally—that is, think creatively or outside the box. If you have exhausted all the obvious possibilities and don't know where else to go, use your imagination and view the problem from a new perspective.

Can I Solve Them by Myself?

If you investigate these mysteries on your own, the clues section will serve as your guide. Once you have read all the clues, your goal is to come up with a satisfying solution that fits all the constraints of the mystery and clues. This process is still fairly open-ended because you might come up with solutions that are different from the one in the back of the book. If you come up with a solution that is more satisfying than the one in the back of the book, congratulations—you are clever indeed! If you have never solved lateral thinking puzzles before, try solving them with the help of someone else first so you can learn how they work. The last 20 puzzles in the book are more suited for doing alone.

What About the Illustrations?

This book contains two kinds of puzzles. The first 80 puzzles include illustrations that show a humorous yet incorrect assumption of what is happening. These are purely for your viewing enjoyment, so don't let them mislead you! The last 20 mysteries in this book are picture puzzles. These mysteries require you to find clues within the image to figure out what is going on. These puzzles are completely self-contained and can be solved alone but are still fun to do in a group.

A Crime in Mind

1.

Take It or Leave It

A burglar robs many homes
throughout the day. At the last
house, he breaks in through
the back door. This house has
more valuables than any of the
other houses, and nothing is
there to stop him from taking
them, but he doesn't take anything. How come?

2.

Safe but Not Sound

A bank robber worked through the night trying to crack a bank vault. As morning approached, he knew the bank employees would be arriving soon, but he didn't stop. How come?

3.

Point the Finger

A valuable signed baseball was taken from its glass display case during a dinner party. All the guests were confined to the study while the host examined the scene for clues. He wasn't trained in finger-printing, but he was able to determine who the culprit was because of fingerprints he found on the glass. Explain.

4.

In Hot Water

A crook rushed into his house and started the bath water. He undressed, splashed some water on himself, and put on a bathrobe. Just as the tub was full, he heard police pounding on the front door. He knew the police suspected him of the crime, and he needed an alibi. How did the police figure out that the crook hadn't taken a bath?

5.

Evident Evidence

Why did a burglar go out of his way to leave shoe prints inside the house he was robbing?

6.

Running Blind

A thief was running from a police officer when suddenly he stopped and closed his eyes. After a few seconds, he opened his eyes and started running again. What was happening?

7.

Hide-a-Key

Dorothy heard that the first place a burglar looks for a hidden key is above the front door. The next place is under the welcome mat, and then under a flowerpot. Unfortunately, those were the only hiding places available to Dorothy at her apartment. What did she do?

8.

Hidden in Plain Sight

Paul found many clever hiding places all over his house for his spare cash. He hoped that if anyone broke into his house, the burglar wouldn't have time to find them all. But one day, someone did break into his house and take his cash. What was Paul's mistake?

9.

False Accusations?

Why was a man accused
of shoplifting when he had
never taken anything out
of the store?

10.

Telling Time

An undercover police officer asked a man what time it was. He then knew that the man was the imposter he was looking for. How did he know?

11.

Wrongly Accused

Tyler was framed, convicted, and sent to jail for a crime he didn't commit. Years later, when the authorities determined who the actual criminal was, Tyler stayed in jail. Why?

12.

Art of Intrusion

A detective examined a large collection of sculptures, paintings, and drawings at the scene of an alleged crime. Nothing appeared to be wrong. A collector of abstract art had notified police that an intruder had entered his home. There was no sign of a break-in, nothing appeared to be missing, and the owner admitted to not actually witnessing an intruder. Still, upon closer inspection, the detective found evidence of an intruder. What did he notice?

13.

Off the Beaten Track

A crime took place along a dirt road. A police officer followed the only tire tracks up the road until he found a few cars parked to the side. Here the dirt was all trampled, so he couldn't tell which car the tire tracks led to. Even so, without comparing the tires, he immediately knew which car he was interested in. How did he know?

14.

Knock on Wood

A spy hid in the shadows and watched. He'd found a gang's secret meeting place, and he hoped to infiltrate. He studied the elaborate secret knock, which was required before gaining admittance. He practiced the knock, approached the door, and performed the routine perfectly. The meeting was still in progress, so why wasn't the door opened?

15.

The Counterfeit Coin

A thief took great pains to steal an old coin from a museum and replace it with an elaborate forgery. The coin was rare but not very valuable, so why did the thief go to all the trouble?

Find Your Way

16.

At the Bus Stop

The bus for Allison's school stopped in front of her
house every morning, but Allison always walked to
school anyway. She was often in a hurry
and didn't want the exercise,
so why didn't she take
the bus?

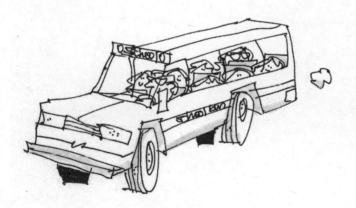

17.

Out like a Light

A cop followed a truck with two broken brake lights. The cop was on duty and didn't have anything more important to do, but he didn't pull the driver over. Why not?

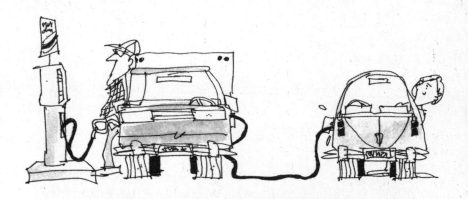

18.

Running Out of Gas

A man filled his truck's gas tank, but the truck ran out of gas soon after. The tank didn't have a leak, so what happened?

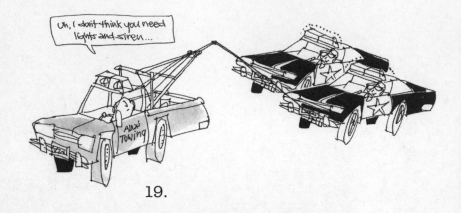

19.

Going Nowhere Fast

Two police cars sped through town with their sirens blaring and lights flashing, yet they weren't headed to a crime or an emergency. The police cars weren't chasing another vehicle, so what was going on?

20.

That's the Ticket

A man wasn't paying attention to the speed limit, so he panicked when he saw a police officer. He had just enough time to glance at a speed limit sign as he passed by. He was relieved to find out he wasn't speeding, so he continued without slowing. But the police officer pulled him over and gave him a speeding ticket anyway. How come?

Now where is that speed limit sign?

21.

Spotless

As a man drove into a parking lot, he saw
that someone had already parked in his
designated spot. None of the other spots
were available, and he didn't want anyone
to park in his spot, but he wasn't upset.
Why not?

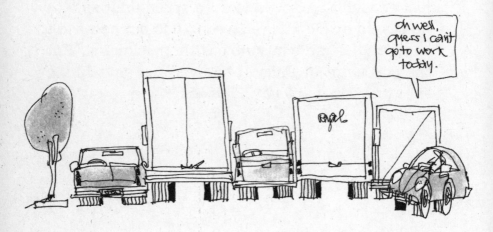

22.

Driving in the Dark

Late on a dark night, a man turns his car onto a road without any streetlights. He continues driving but turns off his lights. He isn't trying to be undetected, so what is going on?

23.

Denied Passage

Only certain persons were allowed to pass through a roadblock. When I tried to pass through, I was told to turn around. How come?

Breaking the Speed Limit

The speedometer on Charlie's car was broken, and he didn't know how fast he was traveling on the freeway. He saw a cop aim his radar toward his car, but he kept going the same speed. His car was going quite fast, so why didn't he slow down just to be safe?

25.

Going Green

Four cars are approaching the same intersection from different directions. Due to a glitch, all the traffic lights are green. How is an accident avoided?

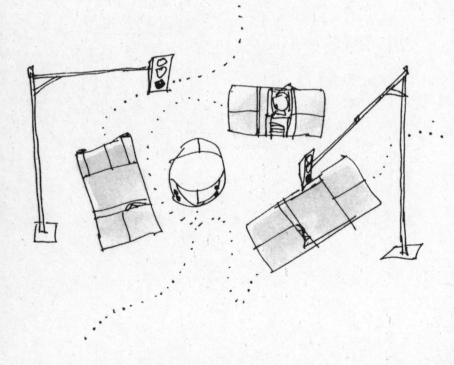

Time After Time

26.

Question of Time

While Matt's mom was shopping in an antique store, Matt wandered around and found a clock.

"Hey Mom, what time is it when the big arrow is pointing at the one and the little arrow is pointing at the eleven?"

His mom glanced at her wristwatch. "Well, that means it is 11:05, but that clock must not be set correctly."

What is the correct time?

27.

Buying Time

Two boys stood outside a store. "Did you remember to ask the checker what time it was when you bought this?"

"Oh man, I forgot, but we can find out with this." What did he get from the store?

28.

It's Only a Matter of Time

A clue read, "At noon and no earlier, you will be shown where to find the next clue."

The kids at the birthday party were bummed that they couldn't continue their treasure hunt. They sat and stared at the clock until suddenly one of the kids shouted, "We don't have to wait! I know where the clue is now!"

How did he know where to find the next clue when it wasn't time yet?

29.

Time and Again

A man set all his clocks to exactly the same time. Nothing was wrong with any of his clocks, but he soon noticed that they displayed different times. What happened?

30.

One More Time

"What time is it?" a boy asked.

His friend looked at his watch and said, "Quarter to one."

A little while later the boy asked, "What is the time now?"

"Twelve forty-five," his friend answered. The watch wasn't broken, so what happened?

31.

Timing Is Everything

A woman checked her voice mail when she came home and found a message from her daughter.

"Hey Mom, the movie starts in a couple minutes. Could you pick me up in two hours at the mall? Thanks. Bye!"

The correct time had never been set in her voice mailbox, so she had no idea when her daughter had left the message. Her daughter didn't have a cell phone, so what did the mother do?

32.

No Time to Wait

I entered the crowded waiting area in the restaurant and listened to the conversation between the hostess and the person in front of me. "How long is the wait?" he asked.

"About an hour," she replied.

I didn't have a reservation and hadn't been waiting for a seat, yet my family was seated immediately. How come?

33.

Times Are Changing

A man looked at his clock, and the digital display read 10:47. A few minutes later he looked again, and it read 10:44. His clock didn't have a timer on it. What was going on?

34.

No Time like the Present

A woman was planning on waiting till Christmas to open her present but was forced to open it early. Why couldn't she wait?

35.

Time Is Up

A young mother woke up in the night, and the only thing she could see was the glow of the numbers on her digital clock. The clock read 10:21, but she knew her young daughter must have turned the clock upside down and that it was actually 12:01. She didn't go to bed after 10:21, so how did she know?

Making Sense

36.

Bird's-Eye View

While two brothers were playing outside, a bird landed on a branch in the tree in their backyard. They could both see the bird perfectly well, but they decided one of them needed glasses. How come?

37.

Eye-Opener

A man had poor eyesight and needed prescription glasses to be able to see. One day he walked into a room and could suddenly see better without his glasses than with them. How is this possible?

38.

Sudden Blindness

A woman was enjoying her tour and the view when suddenly everything disappeared. She could still see, but her view was gone. She couldn't do anything to see it the same way again. How come?

39.

Turn Up the Music

Why does a man turn the volume all the way up on his car stereo when he arrives home each night?

40.

Sensory Deprivation

A man steps inside a sealed and insulated box and is completely isolated from sights, sounds, smells, and the outside temperature. With his five senses completely blocked from the outside world, how is he able to "sense" what is happening?

Getting the Job Done

41.

Change Your Tune

A street performer received small change all morning, so why wasn't he happy when he received a $20?

42.

Behind Closed Doors

When the establishment closed, the doors were opened. Explain.

43.

Come In, We're Closed

A sign in the business window said Open, but when a customer pulled on the door, it was locked. Why?

44.

State of the Art

An artist dreamed of being famous and making a fortune by selling his art. He was unknown for years, but eventually his artwork became worth a lot of money. He was still alive, but he never made a fortune from his artwork. Why not?

45.

Not Maid for the Job

The maid arrived on time, worked quickly and efficiently, and got all her work done. She vacuumed, dusted, cleaned, watered the plants, took out the garbage, put things away, washed the windows, and left the house spotless. But when the homeowners came home, they fired her. How come?

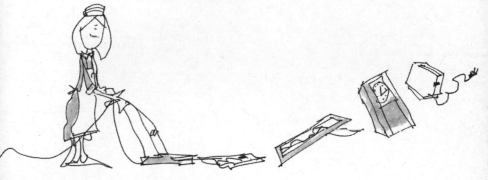

Two Sides to Every Question

46.

When Right Is Wrong

Many things are made specifically for left-handed people, but what is something that left-handed people almost always do the same as right-handed people?

47.

Care for a Drink?

"Are you thirsty? You have to try this!" A woman turned her cup 180 degrees and slid it across the table to her friend. Why did she turn the cup so that her friend would use the same side she used?

48.

Other Side of the Coin

Twin brothers were very competitive and were always fighting over who got to do things first. They agreed to a coin toss to determine who would play a video game first. They had a clear view of the coin, but they couldn't determine who won the toss. They didn't call the same side of the coin, so what happened?

49.

Where There's a Will, There's a Way

At the reading of a great-grandmother's will, the lawyer accidentally dropped the stack of documents. The pages of the will had no page numbers and were now all mixed up. Eventually, through the context of what was said, the lawyer was able to put the pages back in the correct order with the correct sides up—except for one page. If one side was up, the inheritance would be divided one way, and if the other side was up, it would be divided another. How did the lawyer determine which side was the front?

50.

Undisturbed

Becky put the Do Not Disturb sign on her hotel room door. On her way out of the hotel, she noticed some doors with Service Please signs. "Oh no, I didn't realize the sign had two sides," she told Sharon, "and I don't know which way I put it." Sharon was staying in a different hotel room, and Becky noticed that Sharon hung her own sign correctly. Becky didn't bother going back to check her sign. Why not?

When You Sleep

51.

Ready for Bed

A man desperately needed to sleep without any distractions, so he blacked out his windows, unplugged his phone, turned off his alarm, put a Do Not Disturb sign on his door, and went to sleep. However, he was soon awoken. How come?

52.

Letting Them Sleep

A burglar pauses outside a bedroom window in the middle of the night and hears loud snoring. The house is completely dark, and gaining entrance would be easy, but he just sneaks away. How come?

53.

Asleep at the Wheel

A man had to get to work extra early, so he set his alarm for four o'clock. He arrived at work on time even though the roads were full of cars. The roads were never this busy at four in the morning, so what was going on?

54.

Wake Up and Go to Bed

For years, a man woke up in the middle of the night at the same time, only to go right back to bed. He didn't need to be awake for any reason, so why did he wake up?

55.

Sleepwalk It Off

A man wanted to find a way to stop sleepwalking at night. If he started getting out of bed, how could he wake himself up without disturbing any other people in his house?

Communication Breakdown

56.

Dropped Call

Amy was in the middle of a conversation that she wanted to continue, so why did she purposely hang up her phone?

57.

Uncalled For

Aaron called Jason on his cell phone even though he was already talking to him in person. No one else was involved, and they didn't plan on going anywhere. What was going on?

58.

Ready or Not

A man stopped his car in front of the order menu in the fast-food drive-through. Before he was done with his order, he pulled forward. Why didn't he complete his order?

59.

Changed Her Mind?

All day Kari begged her mom to take her to the fast-food restaurant, but when they pulled into the drive-through, she said she didn't want anything. How come?

60.

Talk Is Cheap

A man's short conversation cost him a quarter, but he wasn't using a phone. Explain.

61.

Reading You like a Book

A man was sitting across the café from me and writing. I couldn't see what he was writing on, but I knew what he was writing. How?

62.

Return Mail

Sometimes the mailman accidentally puts your neighbor's mail into your mailbox because you live right next door to him, but why did you get mail in your mailbox for someone who lives across town from you?

63.

Private Messages

Two spies needed to send private messages to each other through the mail using standard postcards. They didn't want to use secret codes, and they knew anyone would be capable of reading messages written on postcards, so what did they do?

64.

Answer Me This

"What were you thinking when you put an empty orange-juice container back in the fridge?" Laura's mom scolded. Laura's response was so witty that her mom was no longer angry. What did she say?

65.

Long Time No Hear

Two deaf strangers met and immediately began communicating with sign language even though neither knew that the other person was deaf. How did they know to use sign language?

Mystifying Mysteries

66.

Lost and Not Found

A man lost a common item. He visited a pawnshop, confident that it would have the item he was missing. He was amazed to find guitars, rings, watches, and many other items but not the one he was looking for. Why couldn't the man find what he needed?

67.

Face the Music

Sean couldn't wait to listen to his new CD. He put it in his CD player, and his friends started dancing to the music. The music wasn't too loud or inappropriate, but a police officer soon showed up and issued a citation. Why?

68.

Show Me the Money

A woman didn't remove the price tag after she bought her dad a gift. She didn't expect him to return the gift, so why did she leave the price tag on?

Oh, did I forget to take the price tag off?

69.

Up a Tree

A family was excited to get their very first Christmas tree, yet the one they picked was crooked and misshaped. Why did they choose such a pitiful tree?

70.

No Fighting Chance

Two men were ready to compete against each other. They were equally matched opponents, but a problem soon arose that prevented them from continuing. What was wrong?

All Washed Up

A woman washed the dishes and did the laundry with plenty of hot water left over, but when she went to take a bath, there was no hot water. What happened?

72.

Straightening Up

After a mild earthquake, a woman straightened some of the pictures hanging on her wall, but she left one particular family portrait crooked. How come?

73.

For Richer or Poorer

Why couldn't a very wealthy
man afford to buy something
that only cost a few dollars?

74.

In the Hole

Whenever a man put his money into a certain hole, he lost it, but he was actually trying to save it for later. What was going on?

75.

Cold Feet

Susie's mom was surprised to find her daughter's tennis shoes in the refrigerator. What was Susie's explanation?

Ask About
the Weather

76.

Weather Forecast

Ashley was sad that it was raining on her birthday and wished the sun would come out. She overheard her mom and dad talking about how it was going to be sunny on her birthday next year. How could her parents predict the weather so far in advance?

Dry Run

A girl started to run inside because it started to rain.
She couldn't find anything to cover her up, but still,
the rain didn't get her wet. How come?

78.

Getting Wind Of

Garrett really wanted to fly his kite, but his mom told him that the wind wasn't strong enough. He looked out the window and saw their flag flapping quickly in the wind. What is going on?

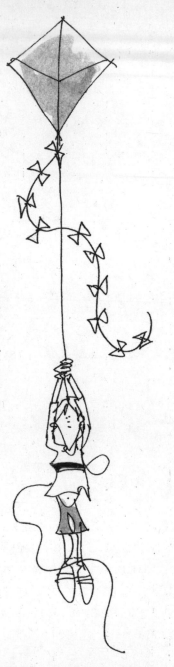

79.

In a Fog

The weather forecast said it would be foggy all morning. Jim couldn't see clearly enough to feel safe driving. He waited in his car for a few minutes, and even though the fog in his neighborhood didn't change, he now felt safe enough to drive. How come?

80.

Record High

In the middle of the summer, the temperature reached a record high, yet people were putting on their coats. How come?

Picture Imperfect

Overview: There is a problem with some of the photographs within this case file. A rookie detective developed the film upside down, so some of the images are reversed. These pictures look like a scene viewed in a mirror in which the left and right sides are switched. For example, a reversed photograph of a married couple would show them wearing their wedding rings on their right hands instead of their left.

Objective: Find the clues within the illustrations and determine whether…

1. The picture is backward.

2. The picture was developed correctly.

3. It isn't possible to determine its orientation.

Method: These puzzles contain all the information you need to determine the solution, so you can solve them by yourself or with the help of friends. There are clues in the back of the book to help with your investigation. Watch out for red herrings, and don't come to your conclusion too quickly because some of these puzzles will trick you!

81.

Photo 1

Is this picture backward, is it correct, or is its original orientation impossible to determine?

82.

Photo 2

Is this picture backward, is it correct, or is its
original orientation impossible to determine?

83.

Photo 3

Is this picture backward, is it correct, or is its original orientation impossible to determine?

84.

Photo 4

Is this picture backward, is it correct, or is its original orientation impossible to determine?

85.

Photo 5

Is this picture backward, is it correct, or is its original orientation impossible to determine?

86.

Photo 6

Is this picture backward, is it correct, or is its original orientation impossible to determine?

87.

Photo 7

Is this picture backward, is it correct, or is its original orientation impossible to determine?

88.

Photo 8

Is this picture backward, is it correct, or is its original orientation impossible to determine?

89.

Photo 9

Is this picture backward, is it correct, or is its original orientation impossible to determine?

90.

Photo 10

Is this picture backward, is it correct, or is its original orientation impossible to determine?

What's Wrong with This Picture?

Something is not quite right in each of the pictures in this section. Find clues within the illustrations to determine what is wrong with them. These puzzles contain all the information you need to determine the solution, so you can solve them by yourself or with the help of friends. There are clues in the back of the book to help with your investigation.

91.

Gone Fishing

What's wrong with
this picture?

92.

Big Time

What's wrong with this picture?

93.

Read to Me

What's wrong with this picture?

94.

All in a Day's Work

What's wrong with this picture?

95.

Home, Sweet Home

What's wrong with this picture?

96.

A Day in the Park

What's wrong with this picture?

Look for a Book

What's wrong with this picture?

98.

All Natural

What's wrong with this picture?

99.

At the Beach

What's wrong with this picture?

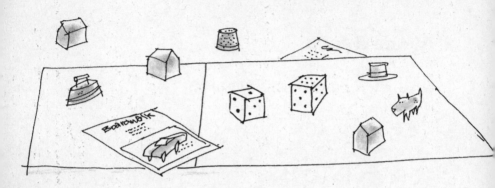

100.

Game Plan

What's wrong with this picture?

Clues

A CRIME IN MIND

1. Take It or Leave It

- He had plenty of room to haul the loot, and he wanted the valuables.
- He didn't plan on robbing the house.
- He made a mistake that morning.
- He was very familiar with the house.

2. Safe but Not Sound

- The vault contents were very important to the bank robber.
- He had planned on robbing the vault, but that wasn't his priority anymore.
- Breaking into the vault wasn't very challenging.

3. Point the Finger

- None of the suspects had anything on his or her fingers.
- Nothing was wrong with any of the suspects' hands.
- No fingerprint samples were taken.
- Something was unique about one of the guests' fingers.
- The fingerprints could have come from only one person in the group.

4. In Hot Water

- The water wasn't too hot or too cold.
- The answer doesn't have anything to do with the crook's skin.
- The police knew he never got in the tub.
- The tub was full of water when the crook was outside the tub.

5. Evident Evidence

- The burglar wanted detectives to find the shoe prints.
- He didn't want to be connected to the crime.
- He hoped the shoe prints would remove suspicion from himself.
- He bought the shoes that morning.

6. Running Blind

- The thief didn't get anything in his eyes.
- He wasn't blinded by a bright light.
- Stopping and closing his eyes helped him escape.
- The time of day is important.
- He was leaving a building.

7. Hide-a-Key

- Dorothy hid her key in one of those three places.
- She hoped the statistic about where a burglar would search was accurate.
- If the statistic was correct, the burglar would never find her key under the flowerpot.

8. Hidden in Plain Sight

- Paul hid all his cash in places the burglar didn't search.
- The burglar didn't know about the cash.
- Paul's mistake had to do with his hiding places.

9. False Accusations?

- The man was stealing from the store.
- Someone else took the items outside the store for him.
- He didn't have a willing accomplice.
- The person taking the items from the store wasn't doing anything illegal.
- The person taking the items was doing his job.

10. Telling Time

- The time doesn't matter.
- The man's voice doesn't matter either.
- The man wore a wristwatch.
- The police officer knew the actual person was left-handed.
- The imposter wore his wristwatch on the same wrist as the actual person.

11. Wrongly Accused

- Tyler was pardoned for the crime.
- He didn't commit another crime.
- He was pardoned after he had been in prison many years.
- He worked in the prison while he was an inmate.
- He liked his job.

12. **Art of Intrusion**

- The art collector immediately noticed something was wrong, but the detective had to look closely to see it.
- None of the art was missing or replaced with a forgery.
- The intruder wasn't interested in art.
- The intruder was interested in a wall safe.
- Knowing whether an abstract painting is right side up isn't always easy.

13. **Off the Beaten Track**

- The nature of the crime doesn't matter.
- The kind of car doesn't matter, and neither do the car's tires.
- The officer was interested in something on the car.
- The car didn't make the tracks he had followed.

14. **Knock on Wood**

- The secret knock was all that was required for admittance.
- He did the secret knock correctly.
- Memorizing the knocking sequence took him a long time.
- He would have been admitted if he'd learned quicker.
- Membership in the gang was exclusive, but who he was didn't matter.

15. **The Counterfeit Coin**

- The coin didn't hold any sentimental value.
- The coin never would have been missed, but he replaced it with a forgery.
- The coin was the only one of its kind that had been found.

- The thief planned on counterfeiting many more of the coins.
- Counterfeits are compared to originals.

FIND YOUR WAY

16. At the Bus Stop

- The bus was for her school.
- She didn't prefer to walk.
- The bus wasn't too full.
- No one ever got on the bus at her stop.

17. Out like a Light

- The truck wasn't an emergency vehicle.
- The driver wasn't using hand signals.
- The cop usually gave citations for broken brake lights.
- The cop didn't know the truck had broken brake lights.
- Under the circumstances, the truck wasn't in violation.

18. Running Out of Gas

- Nothing was wrong with his truck other than being out of gas.
- This has nothing to do with bad gas mileage.
- Although he ran out of gas, he still had a full tank.
- The full tank of gas in his truck wouldn't fuel his truck.

19. Going Nowhere Fast

- Although they weren't headed to a crime, a crime had been committed.
- There had been a robbery.
- A car had been stolen.
- The criminal had stolen the car in order to escape.

20. That's the Ticket

- The sign he looked at was accurate.
- This wasn't a construction zone or a school zone.
- He deserved the speeding ticket.
- He passed the sign before he looked at it.

21. Spotless

- He didn't call a tow truck or do anything to the other vehicle.
- He didn't park in front of the spot or anywhere illegally.
- He was confused but didn't really care that someone was in his spot.
- He was still able to park in his parking spot.
- The kind of vehicle he was driving and the kind of vehicle in his spot are both significant.

22. Driving in the Dark

- The night is pitch black without his headlights on.
- He is lost and doesn't know the road very well.
- He is trying to drive as safely as possible.
- Having the lights on was making it hard to see.
- He was looking at a map.

23. **Denied Passage**

- This wasn't a border crossing, and I didn't need any documentation.
- Most people were allowed to pass.
- People needed something in particular to be allowed through the roadblock.
- If I'd been prepared, I could have passed.
- I could easily get what I needed to pass through.

24. **Breaking the Speed Limit**

- Charlie wasn't behind another vehicle.
- His speedometer wasn't the only thing broken.
- His car was behind another vehicle.
- He wasn't driving.
- He wasn't riding in his car.

25. **Going Green**

- The traffic lights don't change.
- The drivers don't realize that the other cars aren't intending to stop.
- All four cars slow down and stop.
- Think about what else happens when traffic has a green light.
- There were a lot of pedestrians around.

TIME AFTER TIME

26. **Question of Time**

- The old clock was set correctly.

- His mom's wristwatch was also set correctly.
- The little hand on the clock wasn't pointing at the eleven.
- Matt didn't know how to read the numbers on the clock.
- The clock had letters on it.

27. **Buying Time**

- He didn't buy something that told time.
- What he bought is irrelevant.
- He received something else that helped him determine the time.

28. **It's Only a Matter of Time**

- The kids didn't have to wait till noon to find the next clue.
- They had to determine what would happen at noon.
- They were looking at an analog clock.
- The kid figured out what was going to show them the next clue.

29. **Time and Again**

- He set every clock in his house to 12:00 p.m.
- The power didn't go out, and nothing was unusual about any of the clocks.
- He had a big house.
- He made a mistake.

30. **One More Time**

- The answer has nothing to do with time zones or setting clocks back.
- The friend read the same watch, and time did pass.

- The time of day is irrelevant.
- They weren't measuring time in hours.

31. **Timing Is Everything**

- The correct time hadn't been set, so the phone displayed an incorrect time.
- Comparing the incorrect time to the current time wouldn't help.
- The mom made a phone call.
- She didn't call her daughter's friend or the theater.
- She called and left a message for herself.

32. **No Time to Wait**

- We weren't seated in the bar.
- Everyone in the waiting area was there before us.
- There wasn't anything special about us.
- Lots of tables were available.
- Everyone else in the waiting area had to wait an hour.

33. **Times Are Changing**

- The clock wasn't counting down or running in reverse, and he didn't change it.
- Nothing was wrong with his clock.
- There was only one clock.
- The first number wasn't the time of day.
- He was in his car and had just started it.

34. **No Time like the Present**

- The person who gave her the present wasn't there.

- She didn't know what the present was.
- She had to open the present or she wouldn't be able to have it.
- She had to open the present because of security regulations.
- She was travelling.

35. Time Is Up

- The reason she woke up doesn't matter.
- It was dark before she went to bed.
- The clock was flashing.
- The power had gone out and come back on.

MAKING SENSE

36. Bird's-Eye View

- The bird looked exactly the same to each of them.
- Whether the bird was coming or going doesn't matter.
- Neither boy wore glasses.
- The bird was really far away, but they could see the bird perfectly.
- They took turns looking at the bird.

37. Eye-Opener

- He didn't get eye surgery.
- He didn't have prescription sunglasses.
- His glasses didn't break.
- He still needed glasses to have perfect vision.
- The kind of room he entered is significant.
- He couldn't see through his glasses at all.

38. Sudden Blindness

- The scenery wasn't artificial.
- The view was still there, but she couldn't see it.
- She was looking at something far away.
- Something was helping her see the view.
- Her pockets were empty.

39. Turn Up the Music

- No one else is involved, and he's not worried about someone trying to steal his car.
- He shuts off the car immediately after turning up the volume.
- He wants the music to be loud when he starts the car.
- He does this for safety reasons.
- He has a condition.

40. Sensory Deprivation

- He doesn't use his normal five senses to determine what is happening.
- A sensation occurs inside of him that he has felt before.
- The sensation isn't painful.
- People are often in boxes like this one and commonly feel the same sensation.

GETTING THE JOB DONE

41. Change Your Tune

- He wanted to earn as much money as possible.
- He didn't prefer getting small change.

- Nothing was wrong with the $20.
- He was indifferent about receiving the $20.
- He didn't end up with more money.

42. Behind Closed Doors

- It closed down permanently.
- When it was open, all its doors were closed.
- When it was open, its doors were locked, and when it closed, its doors were unlocked.
- It wasn't a business for the general public.

43. Come In, We're Closed

- The manager didn't forget to turn over the Open sign.
- He didn't forget to unlock the door.
- Other people were in the store.
- People didn't need a key to get inside.
- The customer saw the Open sign but missed a different sign.

44. State of the Art

- He never was the best artist.
- His artwork was worth a lot of money but didn't sell very well.
- The materials he used to make his artwork are significant.

45. Not Maid for the Job

- The maid didn't break anything.
- She didn't throw anything away that she shouldn't have.
- The house was perfect when she left but not when the home-owners returned.

- She made a mistake that damaged the carpet but didn't involve the vacuum.
- The plants didn't need to be watered.

TWO SIDES TO EVERY QUESTION

46. When Right Is Wrong

- This doesn't have to do with an inanimate object.
- This is based on a custom.
- When we meet someone for the first time, we don't consider whether they are left- or right-handed.

47. Care for a Drink?

- She didn't want to share her germs.
- The cup didn't have a lid.
- She wanted to make the drink easier to pick up.
- The drink was very hot.

48. Other Side of the Coin

- They were using normal American money.
- The denomination they were using doesn't matter.
- The brothers fought over everything.
- They couldn't decide who got to flip the coin.
- Their solution caused a problem that kept them from knowing who won the toss.

49. Where There's a Will, There's a Way

- The will hadn't been read by anyone before.

- This was the only copy of the will.
- The paper the will was written on was expensive and high quality.
- An invisible clue led to the correct orientation.

50. **Undisturbed**

- Becky didn't find out what her own sign said.
- She knew the maid wouldn't come into her room anyway.
- Her friend's room was right next door.
- Becky locked her hotel room from the inside.

WHEN YOU SLEEP

51. **Ready for Bed**

- No sounds from outside woke him.
- No one else was in the house.
- He made a mistake during his preparations.
- He didn't have a landline.

52. **Letting Them Sleep**

- Nothing is preventing the burglar from entering the house.
- The burglar planned on robbing the house that night even if someone was home.
- He wasn't planning on coming back.
- The owners aren't going to be happy in the morning.

53. **Asleep at the Wheel**

- The roads were full of people driving their cars.

- Nothing unusual had happened.
- No one else was sleepy.

54. **Wake Up and Go to Bed**

- He didn't set an alarm.
- He didn't have a pet, and no one else was involved.
- A sound woke him up, but he wouldn't wear earplugs.
- Nothing turned on at that time.
- He turned something off that was already on.

55. **Sleepwalk It Off**

- He found a way to wake himself up without a loud noise or bright light.
- His method didn't cost a lot of money or require any special technology.
- He found a way to wake himself up as soon as he got out of bed.
- He slept with socks on.
- A sudden pain woke him up.

COMMUNICATION BREAKDOWN

56. **Dropped Call**

- No one else was involved other than the person Amy was talking to on the phone.
- Amy's cell phone was fully charged, and Amy didn't have an incoming call.
- Although she hung up her phone, her conversation wasn't interrupted.

57. Uncalled For

- Aaron and Jason were new friends.
- They didn't talk on their cell phones.
- They didn't have pen and paper.

58. Ready or Not

- He didn't finish his order at the window or go inside.
- He didn't change his mind or go somewhere else.
- He paid and received his complete order.
- By pulling forward, he could complete his order easier.
- Other people were in the car.

59. Changed Her Mind?

- They went to the correct restaurant.
- Kari was upset.
- She couldn't get what she wanted, but the menu hadn't changed.
- What she wanted wasn't available in the drive-through.
- She wasn't hungry.

60. Talk Is Cheap

- He was upset.
- He didn't buy anything.
- The quarter wasn't 25 cents.
- He had to sit down.
- He was a basketball player.

61. Reading You like a Book

- I heard nothing that revealed what he was writing.
- I could read the words he wrote even though I couldn't see them.
- The man was talking to himself as he was writing.

62. Return Mail

- The sender and contents of the mail don't matter.
- The mail isn't addressed to a house in my neighborhood.
- The addresses are very similar.
- They are only off by one number.
- Even though we don't live next to each other, our mailboxes are next to each other.

63. Private Messages

- The spies didn't use invisible ink.
- The messages weren't hidden in the pictures, nor were the pictures important.
- The messages written on the back of the postcards were decoys.
- The messages were very short.
- They didn't write the messages on the postcards.

64. Answer Me This

- Laura was trying to save her mom from doing extra work.
- The juice pitcher wasn't disposable.
- The juice was made from concentrate.
- If Laura had put the pitcher in the sink, she would have given her mom more work to do.

65. Long Time No Hear

- They were complete strangers.
- Neither one had any reason to think the other was deaf.
- No one else was involved, the men were right next to each other, and this didn't take place in a very loud or very quiet area.
- Even someone who wasn't deaf would have used sign language in this situation.

MYSTIFYING MYSTERIES

66. Lost and Not Found

- The item he was looking for probably wouldn't be found in a pawnshop by itself.
- The man was from a different country and didn't know English very well.
- The man assumed the only thing this shop sold was the item he was missing.

67. Face the Music

- The kind of music doesn't matter.
- The citation had to do with safety.
- The police officer wasn't called to the scene.
- The scene came to the police officer.

68. Show Me the Money

- She usually removed price tags but purposely left this one on.

- Even if she had removed the price tag, he would have found out how much the gift cost.
- Knowing how much the gift cost was helpful for him.

69. **Up a Tree**

- The tree was not artificial.
- They bought the tree at a lot and didn't cut it down themselves.
- They could afford a better tree and didn't prefer a pitiful tree.
- They waited to buy their tree until right before Christmas.

70. **No Fighting Chance**

- The men weren't boxing, wrestling, or sparring, but they were competing in a physical activity.
- If they had continued, one man would have had an unfair advantage.
- Either man was capable of having the advantage, depending on how they proceeded.
- They were in a strength competition.

71. **All Washed Up**

- The hot water wasn't used for anything else.
- There was no power.
- She did the dishes and laundry by hand.
- Her bath wasn't in a bathroom.

72. **Straightening Up**

- She didn't prefer having the picture crooked.

CLUES

- The picture was crooked before the earthquake.
- She could easily move the picture, but she couldn't straighten it.
- It wasn't a professional family portrait.

73. **For Richer or Poorer**

- The item he wants to buy is not important.
- He has lots of cash on hand.
- His money is authentic, local currency and isn't stolen.
- The vender won't accept his money.

74. **In the Hole**

- He wasn't putting his money in a bank or jar.
- He didn't want to put his money through the hole.
- He kept forgetting the hole was there.

75. **Cold Feet**

- Susie had a logical explanation.
- She didn't need her tennis shoes to be cold.
- She knew she wouldn't be able to leave the house without her shoes.
- She was usually forgetful.
- She was going to school.

ASK ABOUT THE WEATHER

76. **Weather Forecast**

- They weren't planning on traveling anywhere.

- Her parents couldn't predict the weather.
- She assumed her parents were talking about the weather.
- Her parents used a calendar for their prediction.
- Her birthday was on a Saturday this year.

77. **Dry Run**

- It was raining heavily.
- Her clothing is important to consider.
- Where she had been is also important.
- The rain touched her, and she wasn't dry.

78. **Getting Wind Of**

- Garrett's mom was correct.
- No one was moving the flag.
- He felt wind coming through the open window.
- They were creating the wind.
- They weren't home but would be there soon.

79. **In a Fog**

- He didn't leave his neighborhood to get away from the fog.
- The weather forecast was accurate.
- The foggy weather in his neighborhood wasn't that bad.
- The fog he was worried about went away.
- He initially couldn't see out his car window.

80. **Record High**

- They weren't trying to protect themselves from the sun.
- They weren't too hot in their coats.

- Their coats didn't keep them cool.
- The location is important.
- It was very cold.

PICTURE IMPERFECT

81. Photo 1

- Is the person on the correct side of the car?
- Where was this picture taken?

82. Photo 2

- What is the name of the diner?
- What do people outside the diner see when they look at the name?

83. Photo 3

- What floor was this picture taken on?
- Does the window washer need his ladder?

84. Photo 4

- Which side of the desk does the computer mouse go on?
- Does it matter who uses this desk?

85. Photo 5

- Can you read all the words in the picture?
- Is something unique about the words in this picture?

86. Photo 6

- What is the difference between their clothes?
- Where are the buttons located on a man's shirt?

87. Photo 7

- What day of the week is it?
- Did someone forget to mark off a day?

88. Photo 8

- Does it matter that the letters are backward?
- Are the directions in the correct order?

89. Photo 9

- Does backward writing mean the photo is reversed?
- Would writing on an ambulance be backward?

90. Photo 10

- What time is it?
- What is unique about the digital display?
- What time would the analog clock show if it was reversed?

WHAT'S WRONG WITH THIS PICTURE?

91. Gone Fishing

- Did he catch a fish?
- Which way should the current go?

92. Big Time

- What time is it?
- Are the two clocks the same?

93. Read to Me

- What book is he reading?
- Should you be able to know what book he's reading?

94. All in a Day's Work

- What are the people doing?
- Are they open for business?

95. Home, Sweet Home

- Is it a cold day?
- Is it windy?
- Which way is the wind blowing?

96. A Day in the Park

- Does the time of day matter?
- Does it matter which way the people are walking?
- Are the people being followed?

97. Look for a Book

- What's wrong with the book titles?
- Does it matter which way you lean your head to read the titles?

98. **All Natural**

- Is there something wrong in the sky?
- What is the most distant thing in the picture?

99. **At the Beach**

- What's wrong with the sand?
- What's wrong with the footprints?

100. **Game Plan**

- Is something wrong with the dice?
- Can the dice be rotated so they look exactly the same?
- Did you know that the dots on the opposite sides of a die add up to seven?
- Do you have a pair of dice you can use to try and make them look exactly like the illustration?

Solutions

A CRIME IN MIND

1. Take It or Leave It

The burglar broke into his own house because he'd accidentally locked himself out.

2. Safe but Not Sound

After the bank robber broke into the vault, he accidentally locked himself inside. He spent the rest of the night trying to break out of the vault.

3. Point the Finger

Matching the fingerprints to the culprit was easy because they were so small. One of the guests had brought her child with her.

4. In Hot Water

The crook made the mistake of filling the bathtub. If he had been in the tub, his body would have displaced some of the water.

5. Evident Evidence

The burglar was wearing much larger shoes than his actual foot size. He hoped that if he was ever a suspect, detectives would compare the footprints to his foot and decide he was innocent.

6. Running Blind

The thief was running out of a brightly lit building into a dark night. He stopped at the exit and closed his eyes to prepare himself for the sudden darkness. He knew that he would be able to see more quickly in the dark and that the police officer wouldn't.

7. Hide-a-Key

In the first two places (above the door and under the welcome mat), Dorothy hid decoy keys that didn't fit in her lock. She hid her real house key under the flowerpot. She hoped a burglar would find one of the decoy keys and give up when it didn't work in the lock.

8. Hidden in Plain Sight

Paul hid his cash inside the things that were stolen. For example, he hid some money in the battery compartments of many electronics around his home. The burglar stole the electronics without even knowing about the cash hidden inside.

9. False Accusations?

The man was stealing from a drugstore that included a small post office. He put small items inside packages and mailed them to himself.

10. Telling Time

The imposter initially looked at his left wrist, but he was wearing his wristwatch on his right wrist.

11. Wrongly Accused

Tyler liked the people he met in prison and the work he did there, so when he was pardoned, he decided to get a job at the prison. Of course, now he was free to go home after work each day.

12. Art of Intrusion

The detective noticed that an artist's signature was upside-down on an abstract painting. The intruder had removed it to get into a wall safe, but he replaced it upside down because he couldn't tell which side was up.

13. Off the Beaten Track

The policeman followed bicycle tire tracks and was interested in the car with a bike rack.

14. Knock on Wood

The gang had a certain number of members. He'd waited too long, and everyone was already inside.

15. The Counterfeit Coin

The thief's plan was to make many forgeries of the coin. When the forged coins were compared to the counterfeit one in the museum, they would be determined authentic, and he would have a fortune.

FIND YOUR WAY

16. At the Bus Stop

Allison lived across the street from her school. The bus was dropping kids off and not picking them up.

17. Out like a Light

Although the truck had broken brake lights, the trailer it was pulling had lights that worked just fine.

18. Running Out of Gas

The man was transporting gasoline in his semitrailer. Even though the large tank of gas he was transporting was full, the tank that fueled his truck was empty.

19. Going Nowhere Fast

A criminal stole a police car while escaping from the police and was now being chased through town.

20. That's the Ticket

He turned and looked at the sign just after he passed it. He saw the speed limit for the area he was leaving and not the speed limit for the area he was entering. Unfortunately, he was now in a much slower speed zone than he had been in before.

21. Spotless

A motorcycle was parked on one side of his parking spot, but he still had plenty of room to park his motorcycle too.

22. Driving in the Dark

Having the interior lights on inside a car can make it harder to see outside the car. He was looking at a street map, but when he turned onto the dark road, he turned the interior lights off so he could see the road better.

23. Denied Passage

I was at a toll booth but didn't have any money.

24. Breaking the Speed Limit

Charlie was riding in the passenger seat of the tow truck that was pulling his car.

25. Going Green

Since all the traffic lights were green, all the pedestrian signals said Walk, and all four crosswalks were filled with people.

TIME AFTER TIME

26. Question of Time

The correct time was 2:05. Matt was having trouble with the numbers on the clock because they were Roman numerals. Matt thought the Roman numeral II was an eleven.

27. Buying Time

He checked his receipt.

28. It's Only a Matter of Time

The kid figured out that at noon, all the hands on the clock would point directly up, showing them where to find the next clue. He found it on top of the grandfather clock.

29. Time and Again

He set every clock to 12:00 p.m., but by the time he'd finished setting all the clocks in his house, it was 12:10.

SOLUTIONS

30. **One More Time**

The boys were timing themselves. The first time was the time of day, and the next was 12 minutes and 45 seconds later.

31. **Timing Is Everything**

She called from a different phone and left a voice message for herself. When she listened to it, she heard the current incorrect time. She compared that with the incorrect time of her daughter's message. Once she knew how long ago her daughter had called, she knew when she needed to pick her up.

32. **No Time to Wait**

Everyone waiting to be seated was in the same group, and they were waiting for a large table to become available.

33. **Times Are Changing**

The car's clock and radio used the same display. When he turned on his car, it showed what radio station was playing before it displayed the time.

34. **No Time like the Present**

She had to reveal the contents when she passed through an airport security checkpoint.

35. **Time Is Up**

The time was flashing, so she knew the power had gone out and come back on. The clock couldn't have read 10:21 because clocks reset at 12:00, and that would imply that the power had come on more than ten hours ago.

MAKING SENSE

36. Bird's-Eye View

The brothers were taking turns looking at the bird through binoculars. They had to refocus each time they handed the binoculars back and forth, so they realized one of them must have bad eyesight.

37. Eye-Opener

He entered a sauna, and his glasses fogged up.

38. Sudden Blindness

She was enjoying the view through a coin-operated telescope, but the time ran out, and she didn't have any more money.

39. Turn Up the Music

The man sleepwalks at night and is worried that he will drive in his sleep, so he turns the volume all the way up so that if he ever starts his car while sleepwalking, he will wake up.

40. Sensory Deprivation

The man is inside an elevator. He is able to sense the sudden change in elevation when his stomach drops.

GETTING THE JOB DONE

41. Change Your Tune

The street performer wasn't excited about the $20 because the person had only wanted to get change.

42. Behind Closed Doors

When the prison closed down, the cell doors no longer needed to be closed.

43. Come In, We're Closed

The door wasn't locked. The customer just needed to push it and not pull it.

44. State of the Art

The artist decided that the quickest way to make his artwork worth a lot of money was to use expensive materials, such as gold and silver. But he wasn't the best artist, so his art never sold very well.

45. Not Maid for the Job

The maid watered all the plants without realizing they were fake. By the time the owners came home, their carpets were covered with water.

TWO SIDES TO EVERY QUESTION

46. When Right Is Wrong

People shake hands with their right hand.

47. Care for a Drink?

She turned the coffee mug around so her friend could use the handle to pick it up.

48. Other Side of the Coin

The brothers couldn't agree on who got to flip the coin, so each flipped his own coin. One of the coins came up heads, and the other came up tails. They tied.

49. Where There's a Will, There's a Way

The paper had a watermark with the great-grandmother's initials. When the lawyer held it up to the light, he could see which side was the front.

50. Undisturbed

The maid wouldn't be able to get into her room because she'd locked her door with the deadbolt and exited through her friend's adjoining room.

WHEN YOU SLEEP

51. Ready for Bed

His phone rang. Although he unplugged his cell phone charger from the wall, it wasn't turned off.

52. Letting Them Sleep

The burglar had already robbed the house and was checking to make sure the owners were still asleep.

53. Asleep at the Wheel

He worked swing shift. It was four in the afternoon, and he drove through rush-hour traffic.

54. **Wake Up and Go to Bed**

He fell asleep with the television on every night. He woke up to the static and turned it off.

55. **Sleepwalk It Off**

He put a Lego toy in his sock so he would wake up when he stepped on it.

COMMUNICATION BREAKDOWN

56. **Dropped Call**

Amy hung up her cell phone because she met the person she was talking to and continued her conversation in person.

57. **Uncalled For**

Jason gave Aaron his cell phone number, and Aaron called it so Jason would now have his number.

58. **Ready or Not**

He pulled his car forward just enough for the people in the backseat to order what they wanted.

59. **Changed Her Mind?**

Kari wanted to play at the fast-food restaurant's playground, which she couldn't do in the drive-through.

60. Talk Is Cheap

After yelling at the referee, he had to sit out the fourth quarter of the basketball game.

61. Reading You like a Book

I read his lips. The man was talking to himself as he was writing, and I assumed he was speaking the words he was writing.

62. Return Mail

Although we live across town from one another, our post office boxes are right next to each other.

63. Private Messages

The spies wrote short messages on the back of the postage stamps. They used steam to remove the stamps and read the messages.

64. Answer Me This

Laura explained that because she left the empty juice pitcher in the fridge, her mom wouldn't have to clean it before making more orange juice from concentrate.

65. Long Time No Hear

The men were scuba diving. They met for the first time while underwater and used simple signs to communicate. When they surfaced, each was surprised to find out that the other was also deaf.

MYSTIFYING MYSTERIES

66. Lost and Not Found

The man was visiting America from a different country. His chess set was missing a pawn, and he assumed a pawnshop sold pawns!

67. Face the Music

Sean was driving his pickup truck, and the dancers were in the back.

68. Show Me the Money

She wanted him to know how much money was on the gift card.

69. Up a Tree

It was the last tree on the lot.

70. No Fighting Chance

The men were competing in an arm wrestling competition, but unfortunately, one man was right-handed, and the other was left-handed.

71. All Washed Up

While camping, she did her dishes and laundry by hand with water heated over the fire and then took a bath in the cold lake.

72. Straightening Up

The earthquake didn't move the picture. The family portrait was crooked because the tripod they used when taking the picture wasn't level.

73. For Richer or Poorer

The wealthy man didn't have anything smaller than a $100 bill, and the small market wouldn't take large bills.

74. In the Hole

His money was falling out of the hole in his pocket.

75. Cold Feet

Susie was tired of forgetting her school lunch, so she put something in the refrigerator that she couldn't leave the house without.

ASK ABOUT THE WEATHER

76. Weather Forecast

Ashley's parents weren't talking about the weather. She thought they said her birthday would come on a sunny day, but they actually said it would come on a Sunday.

77. Dry Run

She was swimming when it started to rain. The rain didn't get her wet because she already was wet from the pool.

78. Getting Wind Of

The flag was attached to their moving car.

79. In a Fog

The foggy weather wasn't that bad. The windows in his car were fogged up, so he ran the defrost before feeling safe enough to drive.

80. Record High

The highest recorded temperature at the South Pole is still below freezing.

PICTURE IMPERFECT

81. Photo 1

The picture is backward. The British flag lets you know that the photo was taken in England. The car should be right-hand drive.

82. Photo 2

The picture is backward. The name of the diner should be backward when viewed from inside so that people outside can read it.

83. Photo 3

The picture is backward. The elevator indicator implies that the picture was taken on the ground floor but why then would the window washer need a ladder? The picture was actually taken on the top floor.

84. Photo 4

The orientation can't be determined. The picture initially appears to be backward because the computer mouse, coffee mug, and notepad are all on the left side of the desk, but the person who uses the desk may be left-handed.

85. Photo 5

The orientation can't be determined. The words TATTOO and MOM can be read either way.

86. Photo 6

The picture is backward. The buttons on a man's shirt should be on the right side while a woman's shirt has buttons on the left side.

87. Photo 7

The picture is backward. Why would someone skip a day when marking off the calendar? The date probably hasn't happened yet.

88. Photo 8

The picture is correct. Although the picture appears backward because of the backward letters, the directions are in the correct order. Going clockwise the directions should be north, east, south, and west. The letters are backward because the picture was taken from behind the weather vane.

89. Photo 9

The picture is correct. The word *Ambulance* is printed backward so a driver of another vehicle can read it in the rearview mirror.

90. Photo 10

The picture is backward. The clocks display different times. The digital clock shows 12:51, and the analog clock shows 11:09. The clocks should both read 12:51.

WHAT'S WRONG WITH THIS PICTURE?

91. Gone Fishing

The fishing line is going upstream.

92. Big Time

The two clocks don't match. One shows a little after 9:00 and the other says 12:45.

93. Read to Me

The front cover is on the back of the book.

94. All in a Day's Work

The Open sign is facing the wrong direction. It should say Closed from the inside if they are currently open.

95. Home, Sweet Home

The chimney smoke and the flag are blowing in opposite directions.

96. A Day in the Park

The shadows aren't going in the same direction.

97. Look for a Book

The books are all upside-down! Usually you have to tilt your head to the right to be able to read the title on the spine of a book. Note: This is true with books published in America, but not in every country.

98. All Natural

A cloud is behind the sun.

99. At the Beach

The footprints in the sand are all left feet.

100. Game Plan

The dice don't match. If you were to rotate the dice to show the same dots on both, the dots would be opposite from each other, as in a mirror. To find this solution, you must know how a die is oriented. The opposite sides of a die always add up to seven, so the opposing sides of a die are two/five, one/six, and three/four. The easiest way to see what is wrong is to get a pair of dice and try to make them match the illustration. No matter how you move around the dice, they will never match what you see in the picture.

More One-Minute Mysteries
You Will Enjoy...

Other Great Harvest House Books by Sandy Silverthorne...

THE AWESOME BOOK OF BIBLE FACTS

A storybook, first Bible dictionary, and gold mine of fascinating facts all in one. It's packed with amazing information, incredible cutaway diagrams, hundreds of illustrations, and short, easy explanations that your kids will love.

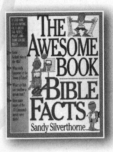

101 AWESOME BIBLE FACTS FOR KIDS

Each entry in this 144-page pocket-size fact book includes an interesting statistic, a helpful definition, or some other noteworthy morsel of data from the Old or New Testament as well as a playful cartoon illustration. These interesting facts will help young readers become Bible experts in no time.

HARVEST HOUSE
PUBLISHERS

To learn more about other Harvest House books
or to read sample chapters, log on to our website:

www.harvesthousepublishers.com

HARVEST HOUSE PUBLISHERS

EUGENE, OREGON